You Make the Difference for 4s and 5s

Using time in the church
for spiritual growth

Mary E. LeBar

Mary E. LeBar has an A.B. in psychology, an M.A. in
Christian education from Wheaton College, and her
Ph.D. from New York University. She began her professional life as a teacher in the New York public
schools. Dr. LeBar has worked with children in many
churches and is now chairman of the Christian Education Department at Wheaton College, Wheaton, Ill.
She has written for many years for and about the
Christian education of children.

Published by
VICTOR BOOKS

 a division of SP Publications, Inc.
WHEATON, ILLINOIS 60187

Contents

Fourth printing, 1979

VICTOR BOOKS
A division of SP Publications, Inc.
P. O. Box 1825 • Wheaton, Ill. 60187

ISBN 0-88207-170-X

Preface

The difference you make in the lives of 4s and 5s is directly related to your own spiritual life. If you are walking with Christ, the child will sense it. If Christ is real to you, the child will know it! If your life is consistent with your profession, the truth will sound clearly through you.

But do you think the standard for your life is too high? It is for you to attain in your own strength, but God is at work in you. He will help you want to obey Him, and then help you do what He wants. Read Philippians 2:13. God has given you the Holy Spirit to be your strength, your wisdom, and your guide. He will empower you. He will teach through you.

Of course you would like to see each child come to know Christ as Saviour. However, you cannot pry open a bud and have a mature blossom. In the same way, you cannot push a child beyond what he is ready for spiritually and mentally.

You *can* lay solid foundations, particularly in the realm of attitudes. If a child learns to love God, he is not likely to turn away from the wonderful gift of salvation when he understands it.

Throughout your curriculum there will be opportunities to explain why Jesus died; what it means to be sorry for sin; and how to receive Jesus as Saviour. However, watch to see that you ask children individually when you sense they are ready to have salvation presented. If you ask a group of children, "Do you want Jesus for your Saviour?" you will probably have 100% response just because the children will want to please you.

The working of the Holy Spirit in a child's heart is usually evident. Then you will want to explain: Though God loves everyone, He cannot have sin in heaven. Jesus came and took the punishment for our badness when He died on the cross. When we tell the Lord we are sorry we have sinned, God forgives us and takes our sin away. We cannot trifle with the Lord's working in a child's heart, but must ever pray earnestly for His guidance in leading a child to Him.

1

YOU MAKE THE DIFFERENCE FOR 4s AND 5s

Because You Know How They Learn and Grow

Through doing more than hearing

It was a rainy, dark, dreary Sunday morning in a city I'll call Meadeville—altogether a miserable day. But I looked forward to visiting a Sunday School department. My first impressions were good because the superintendent greeted each child with a smile. But when the pianist banged out "This Little Light of Mine," I felt differently. Led by a woman who stood (thus towering over the seated children), the 4s and 5s sang the song raucously with various adaptations, including a stanza for each community represented there. "This little light of mine, I'm going to let it shine over Meadeville," shouted the children.

Surely these teachers recognized that children learn through doing, but what a poor choice of activities! The song leader (who should have seated herself to meet the children's eye level) was giving the children a chance to move, but she failed to recognize that the children were singing only to be able to move. The song had no meaning for them, nor was there any reason to sing this song when the aim of the day was thankfulness for the church.

On the other hand, YOU will make a difference for 4s and

5s when you not only recognize that God has created the young child to learn through doing, but when you also provide the right kind of learning. "The right kind of learning" involves environment, content, methods, and the way you organize your teaching.

You will realize that the whole child is reaching out to the world around him. He wants to move because his large muscles crave exercise. He wants to talk, and his talking is more important than yours—to *him*. The young child's mind may be reached through his active senses—he wants to handle and smell, to see and hear.

At the very beginning of the Sunday School hour you plan for a time when a child can talk. Then he will be more ready to listen during the Bible story and other parts of your program. You will try to think of as many ways as possible to make your teaching "touchable" through objects, "seeable" through pictures of all kinds, and "movable" through a variety of activities. You will want to alternate quiet and active times so that no child needs to sit motionless for lengthy periods of time.

Through imitating a model

Recent educational insights stress the fact that children imitate the persons with whom they live. In so short a time as one hour, children can *feel* your love for the Lord, for His Word, and for other people. Your manner in sharing, your spirit in reproving, your attitude toward your co-workers, will all speak of your relationship with God. Children sense all of the intangibles that are an outgrowth of your spiritual life. The children will imitate your words, your actions, but even more your attitudes and feelings.

Recently an elderly woman, a former Sunday School teacher, received this letter. "When I was a child, you taught by your example as well as word and deed. Thank you for your influence on my life. My sister and I always thought we wanted to be like you."

Through feelings more than words

Yes, children catch feelings. And they have feelings—usually openly and honestly expressed. Their selfishness, jealousy, and fear is usually apparent, but so also is their love for you, the one who represents the Lord Jesus to them.

As the children know you and love you, they will gradually feel positively toward what is vital to you. You in turn may reinforce their own positive emotions by your approval. You will be able to direct their love for Jesus into praise and action that pleases Him. Instead of repressing their negative emotions, you will help them change these feelings to positive responses. Your love will help the children overcome jealousy, providing the support they need to face and overcome fears as they learn to depend on the Lord.

And because 4s and 5s are important to you, you will keep your program flexible. You will not feel that you *must* include everything you have planned for a Sunday School session. You will provide routines that give security, but they will be mixed with enough variety to stimulate interest and growth.

Through what you say

You will be conscious of your words and ideas, checking that they are understandable to the children. For instance, when encouraging the children to tell others that Jesus loves them, you will not use strange words such as witness or witnessing, testifying or testimony. You will want to use presession or the first few moments of Sunday School to explain unfamiliar biblical customs and words, following your curriculum materials in selecting what you should explain. Words such as "tomb" and "arose" (used especially at Easter), ideas such as "heaven," and unfamiliar customs such as washing the feet after entering a house, must be taught. Then the Bible story will be understood and can be told without interruptions for explanations.

You will also be consciously literal in your words, because children will understand them exactly as they hear them. For example, a child regards light as light, not as a spiritual revelation. The young child thinks of Jesus as a Person, like people he knows, not as the Bread of Life, the Way, or the Door. If you suggest to a young child that he "build his house on the rock," he will think you mean the geographical location of his home, not his faith in Jesus, the Rock. You will always strive to be concrete and specific, saying, "We know Jesus will do what He says," not, "have faith in Jesus."

Through the eye more than the ear

We say that 2s and 3s need a picture for each idea. And a teacher of 4s and 5s must follow almost the same formula. Fortunately, lesson materials come with all kinds of visuals— flat pictures, flannelboard figures, models, puppets, and action pictures. You will want to use all of these in addition to finding more. A good picture file is an indispensable tool for the teacher of young children. Be a perennial picture clipper! Collect pictures from every imaginable source.

File the pictures carefully so you can find them quickly. (Many teachers do not mount pictures till they are ready to use them.) To set up a picture file, begin with a cardboard carton and whatever pictures you have. When you have 50 or more pictures, you will want to arrange them by classifications, adding more subjects as your picture collection grows.

First, divide Bible pictures into Old and New Testaments. Then organize these pictures according to Bible events. New Testament pictures may be grouped in the following divisions relating to Christ's life: birth (including pictures of John the Baptist and all Christmas scenes), boyhood, miracles, teaching ministry, resurrection, and perhaps a section on Jesus with children. Also include a section for the life of Paul. You may want to group Old Testament pictures in chronological order. As your collection grows, you may decide to add special sections for the lives of some characters—Abraham through Joseph, Moses (including the life of the Israelites in the wilderness), David, etc.

Subdivide animal pictures into wild and tame animals, then into dogs, cats, birds, and other categories as your collection grows. Organize pictures of modern day children into such categories as helping, obeying, playing, children at school, children with parents, etc. Flannelboard stories may be filed alphabetically or by biblical order. Objects, models, and puppets are probably best kept in separate, labeled boxes.

2

YOU MAKE THE DIFFERENCE FOR 4s AND 5s

Because You Explain the Bible, God's Personal Word

You're a storyteller!

The Bible is filled with drama and excitement—God working with real people who experience real events! It contains the deepest philosophical truth, but expresses truth in such simple words as "God is love." The Bible offers spiritual food to people of all ages—even 4s and 5s. Your curriculum includes carefully selected Bible stories, but making a Bible story part of the child's living is all yours!

How do you become a Bible storyteller for young children? First, you must make the story your own. You see it, hear it, and feel it. An then you are ready to begin preparing to tell it. You will want to think through the sequence and action of the story. Then think about the words and expressions. Read the story from your curriculum, for it has been written especially for children. Notice the expressions that are not your natural ways of stating a thought, but are needed to help young children understand. Then practice telling the story for fluency and ease, enabling you to look at the children as you tell it. Eye contact with the children enables you to see how the children respond. If someone looks puzzled, slow up or use a synonym to clarify a new word. There are times when you will want to personalize the story to hold the attention of a child who is easily distracted. You may find yourself saying, "And Joseph felt just the way you would feel, Donny, if you had to go far away from home all alone."

You have done your part in preparation. Now make sure listening conditions are the best possible. Are the children seated comfortably? Does a teacher need to sit between those live wires, John and Barry, to help them concentrate? Does Susie need to sit close to you to keep her from touching other children? Always wait for complete silence before you begin, and do this consistently. You win continued attention by the quality of your telling, improving your narration each week. Soon, attention becomes automatic when it is time for the story.

But the Bible story is not an isolated activity, included merely to entertain. You must pray and expect that the Holy Spirit will work through you to cause the Word to take root in individual lives. How can you best prepare the children to receive Bible truth? You may begin by mentioning a problem typical of your children's problems. In just a sentence or two, you can help them identify with a situation to which the Bible story will provide an answer. If the children have identified with the problem you presented, they will be ready to listen to the Bible story to discover God's answer to the problem.

With this kind of introduction the story has purpose, not only for you but also for the children. When you have completed the story, go back to the problem you presented and let the children suggest the solution, involving them in the lesson application. If they tell what they have learned through the story, they are more likely to carry the Bible truth over into action. Unfortunately, children may be told so much in church that it becomes easy for them to hear without receiving the truth as a message from God for them personally.

You teach the Bible verse as a part of living

In the course of your conversation quote the Bible verse in a context that gives it meaning. Only then do the children begin to "learn" it. What is it you want them to learn? Surely not mere words without meaning, but a thought, and a thought that means something to the children. A Bible verse is not a magic ritual to repeat but a thought to think after God; therefore, it must be used repeatedly in ways that increase its meaning. For example:

"How can we be happy together? God tells us. He says, 'Be kind one to another.' How can we be kind? Let's show each other. As we do something to be kind, we can say the Bible verse, 'Be kind one to another.' "

Or the Bible verse may be a prayer, such as "I will not forget Your Word." If so, it should be prayed from time to time when it is appropriate to the conversation. If the verse is praise, use it to praise God. If it's a directive for living, the children may say it to one another as a reminder, or they may show how to obey the verse in pretend or real situations. Let's not make the Bible verse a mere repetition of words, but a part of conversation, giving it meaning for each child who hears or says it.

Most of all, you live the Bible truth

Do you acknowledge the Bible as the authority for life and truth? Both your direct and indirect references to it will communicate your attitude to the children, though this will take time. Your 4s and 5s will recognize that God gives guidance in His Book, and they will know that you accept and love His Book.

What kind of a book will God's Word become to your children as you communicate it? Hopefully not a book of "do nots," but one that tells of God's love and helps them know what to do to be happy. Is the Bible a book of exciting stories, of warm and living people, a personal word from God? You teach this not only by words but also by your attitude toward the Bible, clearly revealed to sensitive little people who are soaking up much of what they see and feel. They will sense your companionship with its Author, your high regard for Him, and your desire to obey Him. You do not say all these things in words, but in living you tell much.

You work toward the day of personal salvation

It is easy for a teacher to push a child through the steps of salvation. A child may answer your questions in a way to indicate he does want to receive Christ, and express his sorrow for sin, but he may actually lack heart belief.

"Don't tell my mother that I just became a Christian!" *pleaded a college student. "You see, she insists that I accepted the Lord when I was five."*

Most teachers of young children have experienced similar instances where a child has not really understood salvation. You personally cannot bring a child to accept Christ. Only the Holy Spirit can bring conviction of sin.

But do not take lightly the serious subject of salvation because you have an important part in building the foundation that will eventually prepare a child for saving faith in Christ. You will help a child learn that disobeying God is sin, and sin must be punished. Occasionally you will explain salvation simply and clearly. You can explain *how* to be saved, but avoid asking for a group response. Let any interested child see you later. Then deal carefully with that child. Ask questions to see what he is thinking. Pray with him, but avoid putting words into his mouth. Be sure that the Holy Spirit is dealing with him. Then decisions that are made will be real.

3

Because You Lead Them in Worship

What is worship?

One simple definition describes worship as meeting God. You can lead children to meet God, but it is not easy. It is not as easy as talking *about* God or singing *about* Him. It takes prayer, planning, and preparation to bring children into God's presence.

Singing

You may lead your children to worship God through music if they really think about God and glorify Him as they sing. Do your children sing to Him? The Bible-time children did on that first Palm Sunday—but Jesus was visibly present then. Can He be that real to your children now? Yes, at least during some moments of the hour.

"Can we really sing to the Lord today?" a teacher asked her group. "Can He hear us, just as He heard those children on Palm Sunday, even if we can't see Him?"

"Yes!" the children answered. They waved their paper palm leaves, singing with a wholeheartedness and concentration that had not been present in an earlier song that they had sung.

The children showed now they really were singing to Jesus.

Children can worship with songs that glorify God, that lead their thoughts to Him—spiritual songs that 4s and 5s can understand, mean, and feel. But if music is to help your children worship the Lord, you must be careful in choosing songs. Be cautious about introducing new songs unless they emphasize the theme of your teaching and are worth singing over a period of time.

You will want to teach a song throughout a unit (series of lessons centered on one theme) or over a period of several weeks. If you teach a new song one week and expect the children to remember it the next Sunday, you may be disappointed. A week is a long time for children. Teaching a song must be done carefully and well. Singing can be merely fun or it can be much more. You want singing to be an expression of thought and feeling, to be sung intelligently and thoughtfully.

To do this, you will want to introduce a new song carefully. The first time the children hear the song it should come to them as a message rather than a "new song." Perhaps a teacher has been talking about some children far away who have never heard of Jesus. She asks the group, "Do you feel like this?" and sings a missionary song to them. The children have heard the song once. Then the teacher asks them to listen for something in the song as she sings it again. Next, she asks a volunteer to choose one picture from a series of pictures showing children who live in various lands. She sings the song again, repeating it each time a volunteer displays the picture he or she selected. Consequently, the teacher may sing the song as many as six times while the children think of the message and do the activities associated with it. After hearing the words sung thoughtfully as they listened repeatedly to the music, the children would be familiar with the tune and ready to try singing the words. The teacher has prepared them to enjoy the new song and understand what it means.

Always introduce each song, even familiar songs, with a meaningful remark. Do not say, "Let's sing 'Sharing,'" but say, "Let's sing to each other what God wants us to do with our toys." If you are using the song for worship, ask yourself, "Am I and the other teachers really meeting God, too?" The children will sense adult attitudes. You *do* make a real difference as to whether worship occurs through a song!

Praying

Lead the children to worship through the wonderful privilege of prayer. What is your goal? To want each child to talk to God as easily and naturally as he talks to another child or a parent? Yes, but your goal includes much more—to talk lovingly and confidingly, for Jesus, who loves children most, always has time to listen to them. He wants all children to come to Him. He is the One who reproves adults when they turn children away, threatening dire punishment for those who cause children to stumble.

How do you teach children to pray? By example, of course. Before a child begins to pray, he listens to his teacher pray. Your own prayer life reflects your attitude of confidence and trust in the Lord. Your prayers should be simple and direct; it is better to have many brief prayers than one long prayer encompassing everything. Try to have one major thought in each short prayer. You may wish to pray for one thing, close with "Amen"; discuss the next subject and pray about it; talk again and then pray for the next item. Even the youngest child whose mind seems to flit, can pray with you in this way. Your words will be those a child can easily understand, and your sentences will not be long.

But of course you will not always lead in prayer. You will teach the children to pray—in many ways, in different postures, and about many subjects. How will you begin to teach children to pray? First, do not introduce prayer by saying, "It's time to pray." It is always time to pray! Prayer should not come at a set time or be a routine ritual, but it should take place whenever a child or the group feels a need, is thankful, or has occasion to praise God. This does not rule out preparation for prayer, nor planning for it. But you are the one who helps the children feel praise so they are ready to express it to God. You focus on a need and help the children realize God can do something about it. Through conversation, through story, through song, and through activity, you lead the group to be ready to talk to God freely and frequently, just as they talk to other children and adults.

Will you begin with, "Now close your eyes and bow your heads; we're going to pray"? Is this the emphasis you want in prayer—the outward posture only? Or do you want your children to think of the content of their praying? The answer is obvious: "Let's tell God how happy we feel on this beautiful morning that He's given us!" And what if some child does not close his eyes and fold his hands and bow his head? Does this mean he will not pray? Does an outward "prayerful posture" ensure that he prays? Of course not. But will you omit *all* reference to outward posture? Think before you decide.

Why should a child close his eyes? A child is easily distracted by the others around him and can't concentrate easily. So it makes sense to have him close his eyes. But why not talk to the children and win their agreement that it is easier to talk to God with closed eyes? Then you do not need to talk about closed eyes before every prayer. An occasional reminder of why people close their eyes will be sufficient. Remember that the children are imitators. Good examples by other children and the teachers will bring compliance from all who really wish to pray.

What about bowing one's head—is this important? One thoughtful child once asked, "Why do we put our heads down if God is up in heaven?" The true answer, of course, is that bowing the head is a sign of humility, probably taken from the days when people knelt in submission before kings. But what meaning does the bowed head have for a modern child? Explanations become rather lengthy and wearisome. Why bother to ask for it or to explain? Someday the child can understand history and find significance in bowing. For now, why not focus on what he's praying about? (And if you bow your head without saying anything about it, he will likely imitate you anyway!)

What about folding one's hands—is this necessary? Hands do get into trouble during prayer, so there is some point in teaching what to do with hands. But do they need to be folded just so? Or is it sufficient merely to keep hands away from others? Why not *focus* on what you are praying about?

In summary, why put emphasis on outward posture when your concern is for the content of prayer? If the child is ready and eager to talk to God, he won't have trouble with hands, head, or eyes. If you must make posture a major issue, it is not likely that the children will really talk to God freely and spontaneously because they will be concentrating on posture. Young children can think only of one thing at a time.

How, then, will you teach a child to pray? First, free him from thinking prayer must be done sitting in a chair or standing in front of it. Can he pray kneeling? Can he pray as he stands in a circle, his hands joined with the other children? Can he pray while standing at the window, looking out at the snow falling down. Or can he pray while walking across the room, his eyes open to see where he is going? The answer to all of these questions, of course, is yes. Posture is as subservient to the reality of talking to God as it is to talking to anyone else.

If content, then, is to be the focus, what subjects should be included in prayer? It's well to evaluate this from time to time. Are your children experiencing a balanced prayer life? The easiest and most used kinds of prayer are those prayers that thank God and praise Him for specific blessings, along with prayers that ask Him for specific needs. You will want to lead your group to ask for the needs of others also. While a self-centered young child can stretch his concern only so far, his ability to feel the needs of others will grow into real intercession if you do not omit this aspect of prayer.

"My mother is going to the hospital," said Jimmy with wide eyes. "She's awful sick. My daddy cried!" Jimmy looked as though he did not know whether to cry or not. The teacher quickly responded, "Isn't it good that we can tell Jesus about it right now? Jesus loves you and your daddy and your mother. He can take care of her and help her." A prayer with Jimmy was one of real intercession. And the other children felt this kind of need because a mother is so central in a child's experience. They, too, really prayed for Jimmy's mother.

The prayer of confession is more difficult, but you will not want to omit this aspect of prayer. Saying to a child, "Tell God you're sorry," may only encourage insincerity and hypocrisy on the part of the child. Nevertheless, you can begin to teach by saying, "When we have done something wrong, we can ask God to forgive us." Even young children can grasp the concept of forgiveness when taught in the context of personal relationships.

Will you always lead in prayer? No, you will want each child to be able to pray aloud so that the group can pray with him. If you begin this early and naturally, without any implication that praying is unusual or hard, a child can easily express his thank-You or his petition. However, do not urge a child to pray. Remember, he should *feel* that he wants to pray before he prays.

You may also ask the group to sing a prayer to God; every good collection of songs for young children includes some prayer songs. Your group can also decide what they want to say to God, and pray it together. They may want to pray,

"We're glad you love children, dear God." Or a Bible verse may be made into a prayer. A good example is "We love You because You first loved us." Prayer is another way of making a Bible verse meaningful.

On some occasions the group may repeat a prayer after you. Be sure it is their feeling that you express so that they can honestly pray the words you say. Then, too, you must break up the thoughts into small bits that are still intelligible. This is not easy to do. For example, "Dear Lord, we're so glad you came at Christmas as a tiny Baby to grow up like us and show us how much You love us," is far too long. "We're glad the Lord Jesus came at Christmas," is long enough and understandable. Be careful how often you word prayers for the children, however. If you do so too frequently, they may feel unable to pray in their own words.

Another method of praying that has both dangers and values is the memorized prayer. Adults use the Lord's prayer with a sense of unity. A memorized prayer can help the children feel they are a group, too. The shy child and the one who is in-experienced in praying aloud can venture to pray in the security of the group expression and the set wording. Some prayer-poems have value in helping the group express what they feel with words they could not compose by themselves.

Yet the dangers of using memorized prayer are present, too. Perhaps the worse danger is the inflexibility of such a prayer. A child's mother is sick, but a table grace, a bedtime prayer, or a praise poem is utterly inadequate for his need. ("Now I lay me down to sleep" has tragically proved the end of prayer life and growth for many a person.) And if a child has used prayer-poems too much, he feels inadequate to voice his own prayer because the poems are so "fancy" compared with his own words. Good prayer-poems are also difficult to find; it's hard to make rhymes without using inverted word order and unusual or hard words. The most common danger, however, is overuse. Until the children know the poem well, they cannot really enjoy praying it together. As soon as they know it well, it tends to become a recitation rather than real prayer. It loses its meaning, just as the Lord's Prayer has done for many adults who repeat it often. So a teacher must use a memorized prayer with sensitivity, preparing the children for its use each time with a thought directive to keep it prayer (and not using it too much). For example, the children have learned,

> Help me today, Lord, to listen to You.
> What Your Word says, help me to do.

The 4s and 5s have been talking about being kind. Your words directing them to the prayer might be, "It's hard sometimes to be kind. We need God's help. Let's ask Him for His help as we say our prayer together."

If an instance of unkindness has taken place, your directive might be, "God has something to say to us. Let's ask Him to help us hear what His Word says before we open His Book." Then you would use the prayer-poem.

Small children can have a rich and varied prayer life if teachers will work for it. And it is a goal worth working to attain.

Giving

Johnny came from a very poor home. He had several preschool brothers and sisters. He had nothing at home that was securely his. When his Sunday School teacher gave him a box of crayons to use, telling them they were his, he enjoyed feeling they belonged to him exclusively. When a new child tried to take the box, Johnny clutched it and cried, "It's mine—all mine!" An adult visitor would have decided that the teacher was not teaching Christian principles when she let Johnny keep the crayons. But the teacher knew Johnny had to feel ownership before he could truly share and give.

Strange as it may seem, the first step in giving is to possess—

to feel that something belongs exclusively to the individual or the group. It takes a degree of maturity to be willing to release what one has in order to give it to another. Sometimes babies will play a game of giving and receiving, handing over a toy and chuckling when it is given back to them. But this is not real giving; the baby has no idea of really giving up his toy.

Usually, even real giving has mixed motives. Does a child give because the adult's approval means more than the possession? Does he fear disapproval if he does not give? Yes, a child's first giving probably does come from such motives, which is natural. But what is your ultimate aim in asking him to give? Perhaps you would say, "I want him to give without consideration of return, in response to God's love." This kind of giving is hard even for adults! Do not be too hard on the small child, then, but lead him along as he is able to grow in giving.

When should giving become part of Sunday School? Giving money in church is usually a process of transfer—from parent to child to offering receptacle. Is this real giving? Perhaps on the part of the parent it is, but not for the child. Will you then omit an offering? No, for at some point a young child begins to realize that money can be turned into objects he prizes or it can be kept for other purposes of his own. Therefore, Christian educators feel it is wise to let a child establish a good habit of bringing money to church at an early age. However, the thinking teacher will never be satisfied with this as a continued state of affairs. She will pray and teach to help that child *want* to give as his personal response to the Lord.

As you begin by teaching about God, the original and greatest Giver, you are building an emotional response of love and gratitude to Him. Then the child can truly give. Yes, even your youngest child can want to give because he loves God. But the process is not quite as easy or fast as the words on this page might lead you to believe. It takes persistent, consistent teaching to help children understand what actually happens to the money they give in Sunday School.

Nancy was a typical four-year-old, believing literally what her Sunday School teacher said. One day Nancy's mother saw her take a coin and throw it up into the air, saying, "Here, God." When the money fell to the ground, Nancy began to cry. After a few minutes, Nancy explained sadly, "Teacher says we give our money to God, but God doesn't want mine."

How unfortunate it was that Nancy's teacher didn't say, instead, that the money was being given for the Lord's work, explaining what this work is. All young children need help in understanding that the "Lord's work" or "money for Jesus" means specific needs here and now. You will want to help your children realize that their money, given because they love Jesus, helps pay for lights, heat, the caretaker, equipment in their room, Sunday School papers and books, and money to send teachers to children far away, helping these children learn about Jesus. Step by step, help your children understand that the treasurer (or other designated individual) takes the money to the bank. He then writes a check to pay for the specific items you have described to your children.

Money may be the most easily explained way for children to give, but it is not the only way you will teach them to give. If you will arrange for the children to give real objects (toys, clothing, food), they can better experience giving. Investigate the needs of missions, children's homes, nursing homes, and state schools for children. Many institutions welcome gifts your children can give. Something the children can see and value, helps them experience true giving. These tangible possessions, given for another's good, make even more of an impression than knowing the money is used to pay for heat.

What about giving for missions? As travel and TV have broadened a child's world, he can better understand the needs of children far away to hear about Jesus. But you will want to remember that your children will learn more about missions by identifying with one or two people. If at all possible, present one child who needs a Sunday School, a teacher or preacher, or a Bible. Or an individual missionary can become a very important person to your 4s and 5s. Display the missionary's picture. When the missionary is home on furlough, encourage him or her to visit the department.

If you provide receptacles for *both* the missionary offering and for your church, your children will keep a better balance in their giving. As with the church offering, try to present specific missionary needs, such as books, crayons, and other materials requested by the missionary.

Stewardship involves all of a Christian's life. Because this is true, you will want to teach your children to care for their room and its equipment, to hang up coats, to help store supplies, and to take care of such things as puzzles, crayons, and blocks. As you help children know the caretaker and understand his work, they will want to do their part to help him care for the building. Even 4s and 5s can learn to wipe their feet on the mat, pick up papers in the rooms, and avoid spilling finger paints or marking walls and tables with crayons. Small acts of this kind build larger concepts of responsibility.

4

Because You Help Them Express What They Have Learned

With handwork

A child clutched his handwork as he left Sunday School. The adult visitor asked, "What did you make?" The boy held up his paper for an answer. "What is it about?" asked the adult. But the child only looked surprised and said, "I don't know." Undiscouraged, the visitor questioned a second and third child, but the answer was the same. Yes, the children had expressed themselves through handwork, but it had been without meaning.

In another Sunday School a mother reported to the teacher about the value of her son's handwork. "Remember that picture of Jesus that Jamie made last week? Well, he insists that we keep it on the fireplace mantel. He wants everyone to see it. He says, 'Jesus loves us all the time.' "

Handwork may be a waste of time and money, or it may be valuable. Which will you make it? And how? It can be useful in teaching if it reinforces the ideas in the lesson, or reviews the Bible story, or makes the ideas clearer. But it is not useful in these ways automatically. Handwork may also express the children's feelings or provide an outlet for their response to

Bible truth. But this, too, is not automatic. On rare occasions, handwork will precede the Bible story—when it helps teach an essential new word or idea that will be in the story. Usually, however, handwork comes after the Bible story, helping work out the day's aim in relationship to the child's own response. It is part of the "lesson application."

To make the handwork meaningful, you will need to introduce it carefully, remembering its purpose. Are your children coloring or cutting a picture of a tomb at Easter? If so, it will help the children know ahead of time what the word "tomb" means, how it may have looked, etc. Surely the children will be helped if they understand why a large stone was rolled across the doorway of the tomb where Jesus' body was placed—because there was no door to close.

As the children complete their handwork, you will find it easy to talk about its purpose if you have thought about it ahead of time. If there is time to play with the handwork, you will do so rather than stressing the "nice" work the children did.

Do your children have trouble with handwork? Do you find it easier to prepare the completed handwork yourself? If so, examine the handwork carefully. Is it too difficult for your children? Are you issuing too many directives at once? Are you not giving enough direction? One good way to help children is to make the handwork with them, everyone doing one step at a time so that each child knows what to do.

Many handwork activities need little direction from the teacher. But if a paper must be cut at some particular place, it is wise to be sure each child has his finger on the right place *before* you give him a pair of scissors. Once you have distributed crayons and scissors, it is futile to try to get the children's attention. Young children act on the assumption that materials call for immediate action!

You will want to remember that all 4s and 5s do not have

well-developed small muscles. In fact, there may be a great difference between a young four and an old five. Try to commend effort, not skill. You are not as concerned about the appearance of a finished project as you are with what the child sees in it—what is it saying to him?

If you commend Alice's "fine work," how will Bobby, who is all thumbs, feel about his work? After all, it is not his fault that he can't control the rate of his physical development. And even when a child cannot produce "fine work," he can often recognize that someone else's work looks prettier or neater, and this may make him feel inadequate. But you want each child to feel satisfied with his own work, and your commendation for effort—not appearance—will help him feel satisfied. Of course, when handwork is too difficult for your children, you need to do the part that would cause actual failure, such as cutting out some object with rounded lines or small parts. Be careful not to help unless absolutely necessary, however. A teacher's skilled work makes the child feel his work is quite poor, and he may develop a habit of saying, "I can't." When this occurs, the handwork loses both its pleasure and its purpose.

Discuss with the children what they will do with their handwork when they get it home. Where will they put it? What will they say about it? If you help your children visualize what they will do with their handwork after Sunday School, you will have helped them carry the value of the handwork and the lesson aim into their homes.

With playing Bible stories

Playing or pretending is a natural way for young children to learn about other people and personal relationships. Your children play Sunday School, they play house, and they play at occupations they observe—fireman, doctor, policeman. While the children are playing these roles, they are taking their parts very seriously, feeling like the characters they are portraying. Imagination is a powerful force in the young child's life. He can quickly change from the role of one character to that of another.

Can a young child's active imagination be used in teaching him Bible truth? Yes, it surely can! After the children have heard the Bible story, encourage them to play it. As a usual procedure, all 4s and 5s will want to play the story, so there are no children sitting and watching. Everyone is involved. For example, if you play the story of Baby Moses, do not limit your "cast of characters" to one mother, one Miriam, and one princess. There can be 15 mothers (boys as well as girls) all at once, who rapidly change into 15 Miriams guarding the baby, and then 15 princesses who discover the baby in the basket. (Unless you designate some specific roles to boys and others to girls, your children will find no problem with a boy taking the part of a woman or girl character, and a girl pretending to be a king.)

Since the children will experience the feelings and actions of the person being portrayed, do not have them pretend to be the "bad" characters—the wicked Pharaoh, the robbers in the story of the Good Samaritan, the wicked Goliath. You do not want your children to identify with evil acts or feelings, but to feel the role of people who pleased the Lord. Another good rule to follow is to avoid having a child play the part of Jesus when playing Bible stories about the Lord. If a child asks to do so, explain, "None of us can pretend to be Jesus."

Playing the Bible story is also excellent review. And along with the playing comes physical activity which the children need. Because doing is a child's chief method of learning, your teaching can be done effectively and happily while letting the children also utilize large muscles in movement. How much more valuable this is than merely having the children stand up and go through exercises (such as touching their toes) when they can no longer sit quietly. For example, everyone can be Joseph obeying his father by going on a long trip to find his brothers. The children can walk, and walk, and walk, enjoying the activity and feeling with Joseph.

Bible stories can also be played through action rhymes, which call for rhythmic activity and chanted words. For example, the group may sit backward, rowing in their chairs, as they chant (or listen the teacher),

> *Fish*ermen *four* went *fish*ing one *night,*
> *Rowed* in their *boats* with *all* of their *might,*
> *Threw* out their *nets* in the *wa*ter, swish, *swish,*
> *Pulled* out their *nets,* but they *caught* not one *fish.*
> *Fish*ing, they *threw* and *pulled* nets some *more.*
> *Shoul*ders and *backs* and *arms* soon were *sore.*
> *Then* Jesus *told* them, "Once *more,* throw the *net.*"
> *And* they o*beyed,* hoping *one* fish to *get.*
> *This* time the *net* took *four* men to *pull.*
> *Fish* piled up *high* till *both* boats were *full*!

With playing modern day stories

Often, stories of children living "here and now" help apply the Bible truth. Fours and fives can pantomime a story as the teacher tells it. They can listen to the teacher describe a situation and then show what they would do.

You could begin such a story by saying, "Jimmy is playing with some blocks. Margie pulls most of the blocks Jimmy hasn't used over to her building. Jimmy doesn't have enough left to finish his building. Who will be Jimmy? Show us what you would do."

After finding out what one child would do, invite someone else to show what he or she would do. This role play can be repeated several times to explore various solutions. Discuss the possible solutions, helping the children evaluate them in the light of Bible teaching. Playing stories gives young children help in seeing how Bible truth relates to their lives.

Think of the Bible story of Joseph, who obeyed his father by going far away to find his brothers. How are *your* children expected to obey? What hard things are they asked to do? If you want to make your teaching really effective for such a lesson, you will telephone some parents to discover how they expect their children to obey and what things are hard for the children to do.

Playing a story also helps a child carry over Bible truth into his life. During a unit on obedience, for example, you can send the children into the far corners of the room, where they pretend to play outdoors. Then call the children, one at a time. If a child comes running immediately, give your approval for his prompt and cheerful obedience. Playing such a situation will be of greater help than merely talking about it. When a child is faced with an obeying situation at home, he is more likely to remember what *he did* than what *you said*. Whenever possible, get application into the muscles of your children and it will get into their heads!

With musical instruments

Musical instruments may be used in worship but they are usually more of an expressional activity for the children. The children get involved in clanging the cymbals, striking the drum, or ringing a bell and enjoy the activity, not thinking that they could be offering their music to the Lord. You could make an effort to direct the children to praise God through the rhythm instruments, but this active and noisy expression may not be their best way to worship. However, playing rhythm instruments can be joyful expression if you introduce it carefully and comment frequently on the reason for the activity. The children may play their instruments as the pianist plays music to represent God's work in nature. They can make rippling water, a loud storm, flying birds, and nodding flowers.

5

Because You Set Up the Environment for Growing

Through furnishing rooms for children

Low tables and chairs, low bulletin boards, and low coat hooks say "Children are important. Their comfort is important for learning." If your facilities do not allow for chairs, low tables at which children may stand to work are all right, too—it's usually the teacher who wants to sit down! But if you provide chairs, be sure they are suitable. Chairs that are not the right size for small children result in dangling feet—a situation which is not conducive to maintaining the children's attention. And bulletin boards that are not placed low for easy viewing require the children to tilt their heads awkwardly in order to see—another unacceptable learning situation.

Low shelves for the children's use and care of materials are a part of their training in stewardship. High shelves with locked doors are a must for teachers' supplies. (The danger is not from the children but from others in the church who find your supplies handy when they need scissors, pencils, or paste. Then the materials are missing when you need them.)

Most rooms for children contain a piano, preferably a small one. But a record player can be used, or a skillfully played guitar, or an Autoharp. Beyond the basic furnishings are the delightful things that you may be able to provide, such as low window seats for a view of God's world or of God's people coming to church. If possible, add attractive curtains that don't shut out too much light, a small podium for the department Bible, a book rack that displays the books well and is easy to keep neat, and a nature table.

Health conditions take precedence over beauty, however. Good ventilation, even heating, and a bathroom nearby are requisites for young children. Lighting without shadows or glare is important, too, for the children's eyesight is not fully developed. A drinking fountain is desirable.

Arrangement of the room is also important. It should not look cluttered but inviting. Put away materials that are not in current use. Plan a place for coats (and in cold climates, a place for boots, mittens, and caps). If a warm, spacious hallway provides a place for wraps, so much the better. Then parents can help the children, and your room space is thereby enlarged.

Everyone aims at the ideal, but few actually achieve it. Probably the most important consideration, next to health conditions, is just plain space—space to move, to play stories, to learn through activity. But even with limited space, the concerned teacher plans for activity. Remember: you, rather than the space or furnishings, make the greatest difference in what actual learning takes place!

Through the intangibles

You establish an environment of love for each child so that he knows he is welcomed as an individual in his own right. He knows his opinion is important, that he can be successful in tasks assigned because you encourage and support and help him to be. You set the atmosphere of learning by the interesting things you place in the room, and the interesting activities you lead the children to do. You also set up a controlled environment so that the children feel secure because they find you will not let things get out of hand. If some child feels hostile, becomes over-excited, or too active, you explain what is allowed and not allowed. You set boundaries for acceptable behavior.

In Sunday School the children began to play the story. Philip was immediately out of bounds, pushing and yelling. The teacher firmly requested that he sit down in a chair near her until he learned how the children played the story together. In a few moments Philip was allowed to rejoin the group. When he again overstepped the behavior boundaries, the teacher asked him to sit down again, saying, "Sit in the chair until you learn how we play the story. Then you can enjoy playing with us."

You listen, you explain, you love, and you set the example for your children. Then your children will grow in love for the Lord and others. Your example will mean more to them than your oft-repeated directives. You, in turn, seek the Saviour's overflowing love to enable you to love the stubborn, misbehaving child when he seems to delight in being perverse. But you are patient, realizing that the worse he behaves, the more he needs God's love. You are patient but consistent, so that he knows what to expect from you and can depend on you. You are patient but firm, knowing he has not had such training at home, perhaps, and must learn a new way of behaving. You pray much for this child.

Through home contacts

Whenever you can, you try to help your children through reaching their parents, making your visit not a duty but a joy. Let the child show you his pet, his favorite toys, his sandbox, or the vacant lot where he plays with sticks and stones. Your concern will impress the child's parents. If possible, also call on them when their child is at kindergarten or play. Sometimes parents will confide in you, sharing problems they face with their child. Then you may be able to work on some of these problems through the Sunday School lessons. At least you can tell parents your Sunday School goals and invite their cooperation.

If you are having some difficulty with their child, by all means admit it. Ask for their help, carrying the burden of responsibility for the child's problem yourself. You could say, "What do you suggest I do when Ann is too shy to participate?" One teacher did just that and heard the mother reply, "That's surprising! Ann goes through the whole Sunday School hour at home." The teacher was relieved to hear that the child evidently enjoyed Sunday School and was learning. The mother made this suggestion, "I think if you took Ann's hand and led her into some of the activities, she would join in." The teacher thanked the mother and followed her suggestion. And it worked!

Or perhaps you will find yourself asking, "What should I do when Rob keeps pushing other children?" Sometimes your admission frees the parent to admit he doesn't know what to do with the child either. Together you can plan a way to deal with the child or seek help together from someone who knows more about child behavior. Some Sunday School classes for parents or young adults have found it gratifying to spend an evening on the subject of biblical discipline or other topics related to their children. Because they have the child at home most of the week and for the most significant hours, it is important to work with parents in giving any help possible. You cannot do the whole job of laying a spiritual foundation in one hour a week—the Sunday School hour.

You may also be able to help parents use the child's workbook at home—each week or at the end of the quarter, depending on the type of workbook included in your curriculum.

Some parents will need only a suggestion to begin this important activity, but others will need some definite suggestions as to when and how to do it. You may suggest, "If you have Rob alone in the afternoon when the baby is asleep, you and he could enjoy doing his workbook. If you set aside time to work with Rob, he'll know how much you love him even though there is a new baby brother, and you'll grow closer to each other."

6

Because You Are
a Growing Teacher

Teaching need never be dull or routine if you are a growing teacher. Is there any teacher who really "knows it all"? Doesn't every teacher need to grow in his knowledge of God, the Bible, and children?

Because each person is a unique individual, any group of children will always be different from any other group. Then, too, the rapid pace of change in our society makes a difference in teaching. Children who watch TV, travel with their parents, and attend nursery school, are certainly different from children who once did not have these horizon-widening influences. What is there about human nature that is still the same, however? Can Bible students provide a better answer than expert educators or psychologists? If a teacher is to do his or her best for each individual child, he or she must always be alert, aware, thinking, and responding.

A teacher has a lesson manual, but many teachers do not follow the suggestions. Some teachers pick and choose, eliminating anything that is new or that needs some adaptation to the needs of the teacher. Should you do this? No, even if your first experience with a new method does not seem to work well, do not give up. Analyze what happened and try again. And when you do reject some activity, do so with reasons that pass inspection. If you work with another teacher or teachers, discuss what happened. What went well? What did not? Why didn't the story hold the children's attention all the way through? If you are honest and open with each other, you can experience the stimulation of exciting progress. If you are the only teacher (or even if you aren't), try recording yourself on tape as you tell the story or lead in worship activities. Listen objectively. Would *your* interest be held if you were only four or five?

Most teachers also have opportunities to attend Sunday School conventions or workshops where they can gain new ideas and think through methods with other teachers; it's a good place to ask questions. In addition to observing children as you visit in homes and talk to parents, be sure to observe 4s and 5s in their nursery school or kindergarten, also. Not only will you gain insights about the children you teach on Sunday, but you will see what methods other teachers are using. (These teachers usually have had professional training, so you may want to ask them questions about their routines, ways of handling overactive children, and standards of behavior.)

One important rule for you as a teacher is, "Know *why* you do *what* you do." Ask yourself, "Is each part of the program meaningful to the children?" Occasionally you can ask the children the same kind of question. "Why did we make this handwork?" / "Why do we come to Sunday School?" / "What does it mean to pray?" / "What part of Sunday School do you like best?" / "Why do we have a Bible story each week in Sunday School?"

And of course you can read helpful books. An annotated list is included at the end of this book to give you some guidance. If you are a new or untrained teacher, you will want to begin with some of the basic child study books, such as Soderholm's* or Gilliland's.* If you have been teaching for some time, read a book like Young's* or an in-depth study of storytelling like Barrett's* or one on the spiritual growth of a child, like Mow's.* From these books or others in your church or public library you can find references to additional reading material. Some of these books merit rereading at a later time. Where there's growth, there's life and movement!

* See "Books to Help Teachers Grow," pages 47–48.

7

YOU MAKE THE DIFFERENCE FOR 4s AND 5s

Because You Organize for Effective Teaching

Through planning ahead

Working with children means using materials of many kinds: pictures, objects, flannelboards, models, paper—everything and anything! You may spend many hours searching for the materials you need to make the ideas real. But because of your love for the Lord and for the children you will not begrudge the time and effort.

The wise teacher, however, will save time by planning ahead. When you receive your manual, look at the table of contents, noting the Bible content and organization of units. You will also want to make mental note of any materials you will want to collect and use, such as nature objects, seasonal pictures, and items to construct a tabletop scene. If you do this, you will be able to collect your materials as opportunities present themselves. You may want to ask friends, parents, and even casual acquaintances what they can furnish. If necessary, you can put a notice in the church bulletin, asking for specific items. You yourself will become a collector and hoarder, but it will pay off in savings of both time and energy!

You'll prepare materials ahead of time whenever possible.

Preparing flannelboard figures may be done in moments when you are waiting for someone or when you are spending a relaxing evening at home. Sometimes young people can be interested in serving the Lord by preparing materials for younger departments in the Sunday School. They can sort papers, prepare bulletin boards, make models, and trim and mount pictures.

Through sharing and teaching opportunities

If there are other teachers in your department besides yourself, it will be necessary to allocate jobs so that each person knows her or his weekly responsibility. Of course, each one will participate as needs arise, but specific jobs and preparations are best assigned to a particular person. This procodure saves time and develops a team spirit, helping each person feel important as a member of the teaching team.

Does the pianist need to practice songs for skillful performance? Then the leader of the worship activities will need to tell her prior to Sunday what songs will be used. The pianist should also be alerted to a new song some weeks ahead so she can play it as quiet music for several Sundays preceding the children's introduction to the new song. The pianist needs to know what rhythmic music may be used for activities, too. The worship leader will plan with the pianist, working together so closely that attention is not called to the piano, which should be only a tool to assist singing.

When it's time for the children to sing, the pianist should not walk to the piano, fumble for the page number, and play an introduction. If the pianist is following the worship theme and ideas you or the children are expressing, she can often tell what song is wanted and quietly get ready. The pianist should be at or near the piano throughout the worship time. The pianist should understand that sometimes songs will be sung spontaneously without accompaniment whenever they seem to fit the children's needs. Strive to achieve the standard set by one superintendent who said, "Miss M—and I 'think' together. When I am leading up to a song, she thinks along with me and is prepared when we're ready to sing. It's a joy to work with her!" (If your department uses a record player or tape recorder instead of a piano, the person in charge of the equipment should know exactly which part of the record is going to be used, or should have a cassette tape ready to play without a long wait or false start.) Remember: your department doesn't need a prima donna for a pianist! Rather, it needs someone with a sense of responsibility who is willing to work in the background, someone who realizes she is also one of the "team members," talking to the children, worshiping with them, helping with the handwork.

The secretary is primarily a teacher, for secretarial duties will take little time on Sunday morning. In a large church this important person will probably check in the children when they arrive, take care of the offering money, prepare lists of absentees to give to individual teachers, and take care of such records as the church requires. She will also order and distribute materials. In smaller departments the secretary takes care of ordering materials, or getting the order to the right person, checking materials in, distributing them to the teachers, caring for the offering, and preparing attendance records. However, most of this work can be done during the week, freeing the secretary to be an active team member during the Sunday School hour. Do not waste valuable Sunday School teaching time by calling the roll.

The superintendent is generally responsible for coordinating the program. She will call staff meetings, lead in the considerations of the meeting, help in a democratic spirit to assign the parts of the hour to each teacher, and lead in evaluation and discussion. In a large church, the superintendent may be coordinating several departments of 4s and 5s; in a small church, she will also be a teacher, but the "lead" teacher in the team, since someone needs to take the lead in teaching and to represent the department on the church cabinets or councils. The superintendent usually should be the best trained person because she then trains others who work with her and who learn from her example.

The superintendent may want to assign one person to tell the Bible story with an introduction and follow-up, and she may assign one person to take charge of the handwork (preparing the materials, introducing the project, and showing the entire group how to do it before they go to their tables). One or more teachers may take charge of the presession materials and activities. These duties may be kept throughout the year or changed with each new unit, as the teachers desire. But each person should be concerned that his part of the hour builds toward the aim for the day. Then he will be able to integrate or blend his part into the teaching of the whole hour. (In introducing the handwork, for example, the teacher will probably refer to the Bible story and its relationship to what the children are to make.)

References in this book to teachers and superintendents have generally inferred that they are women. They usually are, but the staff should *not* be all women! Children also need to see men as models of people who love and serve the Lord. Children of all ages need to associate men with the people of God and the educational ministry of the church. Often a married couple can work together in a department. ("There's Mr.—," a child said to his mother as they were shopping. "He's half my Sunday School teacher.") As your Sunday School recruits teachers, be sure to look for some men who love children and who will work toward understanding 4s and 5s.

8

Because You Provide a Balanced Program

To make this book valuable to you personally, you will want to read it again. Then put together as much of the information as you can and apply it to your department.

You will be able to provide a balanced program by following these principles:

Quiet and active times

Sitting and listening should alternate with doing, moving, and talking. You are aware of growing bodies and of the children's desire for expression. You plan for learning by doing, and you are alert to see when the group needs a change. You plan to listen to all the confidences and chatter of your young pupils as they arrive, and you guide their discussion in profitable channels during the session. You can, in fairness, demand attention and learn to win it. When it is time to be quiet, the children should find it easier to be quiet because you have given them their turn to talk.

Routine yet flexible plans

The children can count on the fact that certain things will

occur at certain times, such as the assurance of your listening ear when they arrive. They know the sound of the piano means it's time to gather for the Bible story. They know where to place their chairs and what is expected of them during the story. They know where materials are kept, when to get them, and how to put them away. These routine matters give 4s and 5s security and ease. Yet neither you nor the children need to feel bound by routines. If a child were to become ill during the story, he should also feel free to interrupt to tell you. Changes in program should always be possible.

Variety yet repetition
Though the Bible story is usually told as all the children are gathered in a certain place, on a review Sunday the group may move around the room to have stories retold in places where the various Bible teaching pictures are displayed. On a day when the children are going to tour the church, or perhaps go to the auditorium to add a poinsettia to the Christmas decorations, all ordinary plans would be adapted a bit. No one session will be exactly like another—there will be variety in handwork, activities, stories, and responses. However, small children need and enjoy a certain amount of repetition. They enjoy hearing the same beloved Bible story over and like to retell it themselves. They prefer to sing familiar songs, and must sing them enough to be able to remember them at home. But you will plan to have variety in songs so there is freshness and application to the current unit of lessons. How much variety and repetition? A discerning teacher is constantly, but unconsciously perhaps, checking for the right balance. Are the songs too many and too fast? Are they so familiar that the children have difficulty thinking about what they are singing?

Disciplined yet free
The 4s and 5s know there are some basic rules for behavior

in Sunday School, but these rules are not the focus for the children or their teachers. Within the boundary set by these rules, 4s and 5s feel free, and the rules ensure justice and happiness for all. Children enjoy the consistency of a teacher who can be firm but loving. They know what is expected, and they receive the teacher's help to achieve it.

Explain rules when necessary, but most of the time let positive activity make everyone free of rules, for then there is no occasion to break them. Be aware of situations that can cause problems, then change them if possible. Remember, for example, not to take objects to Sunday School that you do not want the children to handle.

Reverent yet joyfully active

Talking about God and singing and talking to Him call for reverence. But what is reverence for 4s and 5s? Surely you will not use the word itself with them! Probably your example is the best way for them to learn reverence. Your 4s and 5s will follow your way of speaking about God and to Him. But this is not a gloomy or even a too-solemn reverence. Your reverence will express your joy in the Lord and His active concern for His people, His world, and specifically your life. You will be growing in your appreciation of His greatness, His love, and His personal concern. Is "God" a happy word to your children? Do they see Him as a positive, active Person, Someone to talk to freely and to love wholeheartedly? If so, you have taught reverence.

Childlike yet learning

Check again. Are you using all of the children's senses in your teaching? Do the children hear, see, touch, and sometimes smell or taste? And are their spiritual senses feeling and absorbing the reality of God and His Word?

The pacing, or speed of teaching ideas, should be suited

to mental steps of 4s and 5s. You are teaching new words, new ideas, and giving new experiences to direct the whole child in his eager search for meaning. Children want to learn. They are already busily engaged in learning without your help, trying to understand and master their world. If you walk in tune and in time with them, you can guide their exploration into *spiritual* areas of eternal importance.

A balanced program
And so when you put it all together, a whole hour turns out to follow a general pattern involving all the principles you want to follow. As the children arrive, there are activities to interest them. These activities will usually add understanding to the theme of the current Bible lessons, perhaps explaining worls or ideas to be used in the day's Bible story. All the teachers will be prepared and ready to talk with the children, especially letting 4s and 5s talk about what is important to them—pets, new babies, new shoes, visiting relatives, and family affairs.

The pianist begins to play a song the children are learning or one they will learn soo. The music calls them together for the Bible story. Then the Bible storyteller gives a question or problem to the 4s and 5s, suggesting that they listen to the story to find the answer or solution. She tells the Bible story well—so well that the children love to listen. At the end of the story, the children look at a picture of the story and discuss how the story solved a problem or answered a question. Though 4s and 5s will not recognize it, this discussion is an important means of relating the Bible truth to their lives.

After sitting quietly for the Bible story, the children need to move. Often they will play a part of the Bible story or do an action rhyme about it.

Now they need another quiet time. The piano calls the children to sit down again as you begin the worship activities. It will be childlike worship with involvement and movement.

The children share in singing, praying, giving the offering, and discussion. Then they will go to the tables to do handwork.

At the tables, the purpose of the handwork is explained and directions given. Then, and only then, are the materials passed out. Teachers work with the children, one teacher for every six to eight children, talking about the meaning of the handwork and repeating directions as necessary. Very rarely does a teacher cut, paste, fold, or color for the children. You give encouragement, commending effort—not the degree of skill or the finished product.

Has this chapter described your Sunday School hour? If it has, ask the Lord to give you further insight and guidance as you lead 4s and 5s to Him. If, however, you find the description is vastly different from your program, honestly evaluate what you are doing. Do you see some areas that can be changed? Could some of your activities be changed to meet the real mental, physical, and spiritual needs of children? Ask the Lord to guide you in making your ministry effective in every part of the Sunday School hour.

Teaching 4s and 5s is worth every effort you put into it. Remember, yours is a rare privilege—the opportunity of showing young children the Lord and leading them to love Him!

Books to Help Teachers Grow

Barrett, Ethel. *Storytelling: It's Easy.*
Grand Rapids: Zondervan, 1960, 165 pages. Imaginative reading to help you make stories live.

Chamberlain, Eugene; R. Harty; and S. Adams. *Preschoolers at Church.* Nashville, Tenn.: Convention Press, 1969, 203 pages. Describes grouping and organizing for preschoolers at church.

Erb, Alta Mae. *Christian Education in the Home.* Scottdale, Pa.: Herald Press, 1963, 92 pages. Concerns of both home and church: the child's relationship with God, with Jesus, the Bible, the church, others, and himself.

Gilliland, Anne H. *Understanding Preschoolers,* Nashville, Tenn.: Convention Press, 1969, 180 pages. Discusses the preschooler as a person; how he grows; factors influencing growth; and how he learns. Includes good bibliography and learning activities for the teacher.

Hearn, Florence C. *Guiding Preschoolers.* Nashville, Tenn.: Convention Press, 1969, 181 pages. Excellent education principles and directives.

Heron, Frances D. *Kathy Ann, Kindergartner.* Nashville, Tenn.: Abingdon, 1955, 128 pages. A personal account of Sunday School as seen through the eyes of a child.

Jenkins, Gladys; H. Shacter; and W. Bauer. *These Are Your Children.* Chicago: Scott Foresman, 1966, 152 pages. Illustrations and succinct descriptions of each age level. Secular viewpoint, but valuable for studying children.

LeBar, Mary E. *Living in God's Family.* Wheaton, Ill.: Scripture Press Publications, Inc., 1962, 38 pages. In large print and simple words the story of salvation is reviewed. Then a child is led to see how he can grow in the Christian life.

Mow, Anna. *Your Child from Birth to Rebirth.* Grand Rapids: Zondervan, 1963, 152 pages. An in-depth treatment of a child's healthy spiritual growth from birth till he comes to know God in reality as Saviour and Lord. "How to educate a child to be ready for life with God."

Nicholson, Dorothy. *Toward Effective Teaching of Young Children.* Anderson, Ind.: Warner Press, 1970, 128 pages. Helpful discussions about the teacher, the child, and the teaching-learning situation. A brief overview of what a preschool teacher should know.

Soderholm, Marjorie E. *Understanding the Pupil: Part 1, The Pre-School Child.* Grand Rapids: Baker Book House, 1955, 65 pages. Capsulizes the physical, mental, social, emotional, and spiritual characteristics, and their implications, for three age levels of preschoolers: birth-2, 2s and 3s, and 4s and 5s.

Young, Leontine. *Life among the Giants.* New York: McGraw-Hill, 1965, 193 pages. Secular, but an entertaining child's eye-view of the grown-up world. Recommended to the long-time teacher who needs fresh stimulation.